No Path To Nirvana

Healing Whispers: A Spiritual
Journey Within

Misty Summers

Copyright

Dedication

To those who wander the winding roads of the soul, seeking the elusive whispers of inner peace and harmony. May your journey be filled with light, love and the profound understanding that the path to Nirvana lies within. Like the rivers that carve their way through mountains and the trees that reach for the sky, may you find your own natural rhythm and flow. And remember, if you stumble along the way, just laugh it off-- after all, even the Buddha had to start somewhere!

Table of Contents

Introduction

I n a world filled with constant noise and distractions, embarking on a spiritual journey often begins with embracing uncertainty, as it is an essential part of the process. The unknown can be intimidating, yet it holds the potential for profound discovery. Just as explorers venture into uncharted territories, individuals must approach their spiritual quest with open hearts and minds. Uncertainty is not something to be avoided; rather, it should be welcomed as a sign that you are stepping out of your comfort zone and expanding your horizons.

At the heart of this book lies the profound idea that our life experiences, no matter how challenging or joyous, hold the key to unlocking our inner healing and spiritual awakening. It is a discovery that invites you to see every moment, whether filled with joy or sorrow, as sacred and integral to your personal evolution. Through understanding and embracing these experiences, we uncover the layers of ourselves that have been shrouded in doubt, fear, and confusion.

Our emotions are poignant storytellers; they narrate tales of love lost and found, of battles fought and won within the quiet realm of our hearts. In sharing my own story, I invite you to reflect on your own. Picture yourself standing at the edge of a serene forest, where each step forward brings you closer to a place of peace and self-acceptance. Here, among the tall trees that whisper ancient secrets, you realize that every experience has taught you something invaluable. Even the most painful memories serve as catalysts for profound transformation.

From the initial pages, you'll sense that this journey acknowledges the interconnectedness of mind, body, and spirit. There is no separation between our physical experiences and our spiritual ones; they feed into each other, creating a harmonious dance of existence. This book is structured to guide you through various phases of this exploration. Each chapter is a stepping stone toward deeper self-awareness and authentic living.

In the coming chapters, you will learn how to embrace inner silence, a practice that enables you to listen to your soul's whispers amid the chaotic noise of daily life. Inner silence is not about absence; it is about presence—being fully present to the subtle energies within you. By cultivating this practice, you open the door to unprecedented clarity and insight.

We will also delve into harnessing spiritual energy, an empowering force that flows through us all, waiting to be awakened and directed toward healing. Imagine tapping into a stream of energy that rejuvenates every part of your being, illuminating the darkest corners of your heart. This energy is transformative; it heals not just on a physical level but reaches deep into the core of your existence, addressing root causes and dissolving barriers that hinder growth.

Each chapter invites you to engage with practices that promote mindfulness and spiritual growth, whether through meditation, journaling, or engaging with nature. These practices act as bridges connecting you to a higher state of awareness, guiding you gently yet profoundly toward a space of inner peace and fulfillment. You will discover methods that help you ground yourself in the present moment, letting go of past traumas and future anxieties.

The book also highlights the importance of community and connection. Spiritual growth does not happen in isolation; it thrives in the rich soil of shared experiences and collective wisdom. By connecting with others who are also on a path of self-healing, you draw strength and inspiration from their journeys and, in turn, offer your own insights and support. This reciprocal relationship fosters an environment of mutual growth and nurturing.

As you navigate through these chapters, imagine yourself shedding layers of old beliefs and patterns, much like a snake sheds its skin. With each layer you release, you step closer to your true essence—a being of light and immense potential. The more aligned you become with your authentic self, the more effortlessly you attract experiences and relationships that resonate with your highest good.

Are you ready to embark on a voyage of self-discovery and spiritual evolution? Open your heart and mind to the transformative power of personal experiences as we unravel the mysteries of healing, connection, and authenticity together in the pages that follow. This book is not just a passive read; it is an active journey, calling you to engage deeply with its teachings and integrate them into your daily life.

Approach each chapter with curiosity and openness, knowing that the process of transformation is often gradual and nonlinear. Some insights will strike you like lightning, while others may take time to germinate and grow. Trust in the timing of your journey and be gentle with yourself as you navigate its ups and downs.

Remember, this is a safe space for exploration. As you read, allow yourself to feel vulnerable, to confront the shadows that lurk within, and to celebrate the light that constantly seeks to emerge.

Vulnerability is not a sign of weakness but a testament to your courage and willingness to heal.

By the end of this book, my hope is that you will emerge not only with a deeper understanding of yourself but also with a toolkit of strategies and practices to continue your journey beyond these pages. You will find that the path of self-discovery is not a destination but a continuous unfolding—a beautiful dance between your inner and outer worlds.

So, take a deep breath and step boldly into this transformative journey. Welcome the changes, the challenges, and the revelations that lie ahead. Know that you are not alone; countless souls have walked this path before you, and countless more will follow. Together, let us navigate the intricacies of personal transformation, finding healing, wisdom, and spiritual awakening in each step we take.

Chapter One

The Beginning of The Spiritual Quest

Beginning a spiritual quest often stems from an inner sense of restlessness, a feeling that something fundamental is missing from one's life. This chapter delves into significant growth and self-discovery. By understanding this inner void, we can see it not as a flaw, but as an invitation to explore the deeper dimensions of our existence. This initial awareness sets the stage for embarking on a journey filled with transformative potential.

Throughout the chapter, we will examine various manifestations of inner discontent and how they indicate the need for spiritual exploration. The discussion will extend to understanding the role of fear of the unknown in this journey and how confronting such fears requires courage and willingness to step into unfamiliar territory. We will also look at signs and messages from the universe that guide us along the way and explore practices that cultivate mindfulness and self-awareness. These elements collectively offer a comprehensive roadmap for anyone ready to take the first steps on their spiritual path.

Identifying the Inner Void and Longing for More

Our spiritual journeys often begin with an internal restlessness, a quiet but persistent sense of discontent that something fundamental is missing from our lives. This inner discontent serves as a powerful catalyst for personal growth and transformation. It nudges us toward seeking deeper meaning and understanding. When we finally recognize this discomfort—not as something to be avoided but as a signpost pointing toward our need for self-discovery—we take the first crucial step on our spiritual path.

Inner discontent can manifest in various ways, such as a feeling of emptiness despite external success or a perpetual sense of unease. These feelings are important indicators that there is more to life than what we currently perceive. They encourage us to explore uncharted territories within ourselves and confront the aspects of our existence that we might have ignored or suppressed. Understanding that this sense of dissatisfaction is not a flaw but an invitation to grow helps shift our perspective and opens us up to new possibilities.

One significant hurdle at the beginning of any spiritual quest is the fear of the unknown. This fear can be paralyzing, stopping us in our tracks before we have even begun. Confronting this fear requires courage and willingness to step into unfamiliar territory. It is natural to feel anxious about leaving behind the safety of the known world, but it is essential to understand that growth and transformation often require venturing into the unknown. By acknowledging our fears, we can begin to dismantle them and move forward with greater confidence.

The initial stage of any journey can be daunting, filled with doubts and uncertainties. Overcoming these initial fears and doubts is a vital part of the process. When starting out, it is helpful to remind ourselves that every great adventure begins with a single step, and every meaningful journey involves moments of uncertainty. Embracing the discomfort and trusting in the process allows us to navigate these early stages with grace and resilience. It is important to remember that doubt is a natural part of growth; it challenges us to question our assumptions and seek deeper truths.

As we embark on our spiritual journey, we may encounter subtle messages from the universe guiding us along the way. These messages can come in many forms—synchronicities, intuitive insights, or even seemingly random events that carry profound significance. Interpreting these subtle messages requires openness and attentiveness. By paying close attention to the small details of our daily lives, we can discern patterns and meanings that might otherwise go unnoticed. These messages often serve as gentle reminders that we are on the right path, encouraging us to continue our quest with renewed vigor.

Cultivating curiosity about the source of our emotional emptiness can provide valuable insights into our spiritual needs. This practice involves asking ourselves to probe questions about our experiences, feelings, and desires. What are we truly searching for? What aspects of our lives feel unfulfilled? By exploring these questions with an open mind, we can uncover hidden layers of our consciousness and gain a deeper understanding of ourselves. Curiosity drives us to seek answers and, in doing so, facilitates our spiritual growth and transformation.

Embracing discomfort as a stepping stone towards transformation is another crucial concept. Discomfort is often a sign that we are stretching beyond our comfort zones and challenging ourselves to grow. Instead of avoiding uncomfortable situations or emotions, embracing them allows us to confront our limitations and break free from old patterns. This process is not always easy, but it is necessary for meaningful change. By viewing discomfort as an opportunity for growth rather than a barrier, we can navigate our spiritual journeys with greater resilience and purpose.

To cultivate a deeper connection with our spiritual selves, it is beneficial to engage in practices that foster mindfulness and self-awareness. Whether through meditation, journaling, or spending time in nature, these practices help quiet the mind and allow us to tune into our inner wisdom. They create space for reflection and introspection, enabling us to listen to our inner voice and align ourselves with our true purpose. Engaging in regular mindfulness practices can also enhance our ability to recognize and interpret the subtle messages from the universe that guide us on our path.

Setting Intentions for the Journey Ahead

Establishing clear intentions is vital when embarking on a spiritual journey. This process begins with clarifying personal goals and aspirations. Understanding what we hope to achieve on our spiritual quest sets a foundation for all subsequent actions. For many, this might mean seeking inner peace, healing past wounds, or connecting with a higher power. By taking the time to define these objectives, we ensure that our journey has direction and purpose.

Once our goals are clear, practicing manifestation through intention setting becomes essential. Manifestation involves focusing our thoughts, beliefs, and feelings on bringing specific desires into reality. It is about aligning one's energy with the universe to attract what they want. One effective way to practice this is by using positive affirmations daily. These affirmations can serve as powerful reminders of our intentions and keep us motivated. Visualizing the desired outcomes also reinforces these intentions, making them feel more attainable.

Moreover, aligning actions with intentions is crucial in reinforcing spiritual progress. It's not enough to simply set intentions; we must actively pursue them through our daily deeds. For instance, if one's goal is to cultivate inner peace, incorporating mindfulness practices like meditation or yoga into daily routines can be beneficial. Similarly, if the aspiration is to heal emotional wounds, engaging in therapeutic activities or seeking professional guidance might be necessary. Consistent action signals to oneself and the universe that the intentions are genuine and deeply rooted.

Examining personal beliefs and conditioning is another integral aspect of setting clear intentions. Our beliefs shape our perception of reality and influence our decisions and actions. Often, these beliefs are inherited from societal norms, cultural backgrounds, and personal experiences. Taking the time to reflect on and question these beliefs allows us to discern which ones align with our true selves and which ones hinder our spiritual growth. For example, someone conditioned to believe that vulnerability is a weakness may need to reframe this belief to embrace vulnerability as a pathway to deeper connections and self-awareness.

Final Insights

Embarking on a spiritual journey begins with recognizing the inner void and longing for more in our lives. This chapter has guided us through understanding how inner discontent can serve as a catalyst for personal growth and transformation. By embracing this discomfort, we open ourselves to self-discovery and deeper meaning. Addressing the fear of the unknown is crucial, as it requires courage to step beyond our comfort zones and trust the process of growth. Acknowledging subtle messages from the universe and cultivating curiosity about our emotional emptiness enhances our ability to connect with our spiritual selves, paving the way for significant transformation.

As we set out on this path, establishing clear intentions helps us create a sense of direction and purpose. Intentions guide our actions and align them with our deepest desires, ensuring that our spiritual journey remains focused and meaningful. By consistently examining and questioning personal beliefs and conditioning, we can discard those that no longer serve us and embrace new perspectives that foster growth. Through mindfulness practices and daily affirmations, we reinforce our intentions, enabling us to manifest our aspirations. This chapter underscores the importance of clarity and determination, reminding us that every step we take brings us closer to fulfilling our spiritual goals.

Chapter Two

Embracing Your Wounds

E mbracing your wounds is a transformative journey that invites you to see past emotional pain as an opportunity for growth. Often, these wounds stem from deep-rooted past experiences, traumas, or unmet needs that shape our behaviors and emotional responses. By recognizing and accepting this pain, we allow ourselves the potential to heal and evolve into stronger, more resilient individuals.

In this chapter, you will explore how acknowledging emotional pain can lead to profound insights and healing. You will learn about the origins of emotional wounds, the importance of honoring your feelings, recognizing triggers, and seeking support. Through practical examples and reflective writing, this chapter aims to guide you in transforming your trauma into a source of strength, paving the way for personal growth and self-discovery.

Acknowledge and Accept Your Emotional Pain

Understanding and embracing emotional pain can be a transformative experience on the path to healing and growth. Emotional wounds, much like physical ones, need attention and care. By recognizing and working through these hurts, we allow ourselves the opportunity to heal and evolve.

To begin with, understanding the origins of emotional pain is pivotal. Emotional pain often has deep roots, tracing back to past experiences, traumas, or unmet needs. By introspectively exploring the sources of this pain, individuals can uncover hidden layers of their psyche, gaining valuable insights into their behaviors and emotional responses. When you understand where your pain comes from, it becomes easier to address it directly and effectively. This journey might involve reflecting on childhood memories, past relationships, or significant life events that have left an indelible mark. Emphasizing the importance of this exploration helps demystify the process and underscores its necessity in the broader context of healing.

For example, someone who struggles with trust issues may find that their distrust stems from childhood experiences of betrayal or inconsistency from caregivers. By recognizing these patterns and their origins, individuals can start to untangle the complex web of emotions and thoughts that perpetuate their pain. This realization is not just enlightening but also empowering, as it lays the groundwork for meaningful healing.

Another crucial aspect of addressing emotional wounds is honoring your feelings. In a society that often encourages suppressing negative emotions, allowing oneself to genuinely feel pain can be a radical act of self-care. Acknowledging and experiencing emotions fully is essential for moving through them. Ignoring or suppressing emotional pain only causes it to fester, potentially leading to more significant issues over time, such as anxiety, depression, or physical ailments.

Imagine navigating grief after losing a loved one. The natural inclination might be to avoid the overwhelming sadness, but by sitting with and honoring those feelings, you permit yourself to grieve properly. This act of facing emotional pain head-on fosters resilience and paves the way for authentic recovery. Honoring your feelings doesn't mean wallowing in them indefinitely; rather, it means giving yourself the grace to process your emotions without judgment.

Recognizing triggers is another fundamental step in addressing unresolved emotions. Triggers are reminders of past traumas that can cause intense emotional reactions. Identifying these triggers allows for better management and even resolution of lingering pain. Triggers can be anything from places and people to certain smells or sounds that evoke past memories and emotions.

When you recognize what prompts these strong emotional responses, you can start to develop strategies to manage them. For instance, if a particular place reminds you of a traumatic event, acknowledging this trigger can help you prepare mentally before encountering it again. You might also choose to gradually expose yourself to the trigger in a controlled manner, thereby reducing its power over time. Being mindful of these triggers contributes to a deeper understanding of your emotional landscape and aids in crafting effective coping mechanisms.

Seeking support is an invaluable part of the healing process. Humans are inherently social beings, and connecting with others provides not only comfort but also validation. Sharing your pain with trusted individuals can lighten the emotional burden. Whether it's friends, family, or support groups, talking about your experiences offers a sense of relief and creates a space for empathy and mutual understanding.

For example, joining a support group for individuals who have experienced similar losses or traumas can provide a safe environment to share stories and coping strategies. This collective sharing fosters a sense of community and belonging, which is critical when grappling with emotional pain. Additionally, professional support from therapists or counselors can be immensely beneficial. These professionals offer objective perspectives and are trained to provide tools and techniques for managing emotional distress effectively.

Seeking professional help when needed is a sign of strength and self-care. There is sometimes a stigma associated with seeing a therapist or counselor, but reaching out for professional assistance demonstrates a commitment to oneself. Therapists can help unravel complex emotional issues, offering structured approaches to healing. They introduce techniques such as cognitive-behavioral therapy (CBT), mindfulness, and other therapeutic modalities designed to assist in processing and transforming emotional pain.

Finding Strength in Vulnerability

Vulnerability often conjures images of weakness and exposure, but in reality, it requires immense courage. Embracing vulnerability means stepping into the unknown with bravery. It involves presenting our true selves to the world, flaws and all, which can feel incredibly intimidating. But by doing so, we create paths for genuine connections and authentic relationships. For individuals dealing with emotional wounds, vulnerability is a stepping stone to healing. When you dare to be vulnerable, you also open yourself up to the possibility of growth and transformation.

This journey begins with understanding that being vulnerable is not synonymous with being weak. On the contrary, it takes remarkable strength to show your true colors, especially when they reveal scars from past experiences. Think of vulnerability as a bridge between your present self and your healed future self. Each step you take across this bridge moves you closer to resilience and strength. By acknowledging your vulnerabilities, you allow yourself to confront and understand them better.

Embracing imperfection goes hand in hand with vulnerability. Recognizing that imperfection is an intrinsic part of being human helps dismantle unrealistic expectations. Society often pushes the idea of perfection, but it's our imperfections that make us unique and relatable. Accepting your flaws can be liberating. It shifts the focus from what you lack to what you have. When you embrace your imperfections, you're giving yourself permission to be human. This acceptance lays a foundation for self-love and self-acceptance.

Consider a cracked piece of pottery that has been repaired with gold—an art form known as kintsugi. The cracks are not hidden; instead, they are highlighted to show the beauty in brokenness. Similarly, embracing your imperfections does not mean ignoring or hiding them. Instead, it involves seeing them as integral parts of your story and your growth. Learning to love yourself despite (or even because of) these imperfections can lead to profound personal transformation.

Vulnerability has more to teach us than just bravery and acceptance. It holds valuable life lessons that can shape our future. When we allow ourselves to be vulnerable, we learn about our strengths and weaknesses, our fears, and our desires. This self-awareness is crucial for personal development. By facing vulnerability head-on, we build resilience. We learn to cope with uncomfortable emotions and situations, which fortifies our mental and emotional strength over time.

The journey through vulnerability can be enlightening. Through introspection and reflection, you begin to understand the deeper layers of your psyche. These insights pave the way for empathy, both towards yourself and others. Being vulnerable makes you more attuned to the pain and struggles of those around you, fostering a sense of connection and compassion. This process ultimately enriches your relational experiences, making them more meaningful and profound.

Reflecting on past traumas through a lens of understanding and compassion can also bring significant healing. It is essential to look back not with judgment but with kindness. This approach can uncover hidden wisdom within your experiences. Traumatic events often carry lessons that, when recognized, can transform suffering into strength. By examining your past with a nurturing eye, you can find meaning in your pain and use it as a catalyst for personal growth.

Consider the stories of many who have endured hardships and emerged stronger. Their narratives often share a common thread: the ability to extract lessons from their pain and use them to navigate life's challenges more effectively. When you manage to do this, you turn your trauma into a source of wisdom. This newfound wisdom becomes an empowering tool that enables you to face future adversities with greater confidence and resilience.

Sharing the wisdom gained from transforming trauma can inspire and guide others on their journeys. Your story of healing could offer hope to someone grappling with similar issues. Personal experiences are powerful tools for connection and support. When you share your journey, you provide a roadmap for others who may be feeling lost. You become a beacon of hope, showing that it is possible to move from pain to empowerment.

Transforming your trauma into a source of strength does not just benefit you; it can be a lifeline for others. When people see that you have overcome your struggles and emerged stronger, it instills a sense of possibility and courage in them. Your experiences and the lessons learned can serve as testimony to the resilience of the human spirit. By sharing your narrative, you contribute to a collective healing journey, offering encouragement and solidarity to those in need.

Summary and Reflections

Seeing past wounds as opportunities for growth requires us to acknowledge and accept our emotional pain. By understanding where this pain originates, we can begin to address it directly. Honoring our emotions, rather than suppressing them, allows us to navigate through them safely. Recognizing triggers helps in managing and resolving lingering pain, while seeking support from others provides comfort and validation. These steps are essential for meaningful healing and help pave the way for resilience and transformation.

Embracing vulnerability is another significant part of this journey. It involves accepting imperfections and showing our true selves despite past scars. This courage fosters genuine connections and personal growth. Reflecting on past traumas with compassion uncovers hidden wisdom and transforms suffering into strength. Sharing these experiences offers hope and guidance to others, demonstrating the resilience of the human spirit. By viewing our wounds through a lens of growth, we empower ourselves and inspire those around us.

Chapter Three

Cultivating Self-Love

C ultivating self-love involves embarking on a journey of accepting and cherishing oneself, even amidst imperfections and setbacks. It calls for an intentional shift in how we perceive and treat ourselves, recognizing that the same compassion we extend to others is deeply deserved by our own hearts. Many times, we fall into the trap of harsh self-criticism, which can undermine our confidence and well-being. Embracing self-love means challenging these negative patterns and replacing them with kinder, more nurturing internal dialogues.

In this chapter, you will explore practical ways to cultivate self-compassion as a foundational step towards self-love. You will learn how to treat yourself with the same empathy and support you would offer a close friend. Additionally, we will discuss the importance of embracing your imperfections, viewing them not as flaws, but as opportunities for growth and resilience. We also will delve into the transformative power of forgiveness, guiding you to release self-blame and foster a deeper sense of self-acceptance. By integrating these practices, you can build a more loving relationship with yourself, paving the way for personal healing and inner peace.

Practicing Self-Compassion

Practicing self-compassion is a vital step towards self-love and acceptance. At its core, self-compassion means treating yourself with the same kindness, care, and understanding you would offer to a dear friend in need. Many of us are quick to criticize and blame ourselves for our perceived shortcomings, but this constant self-criticism can be toxic and erode our sense of self-worth. Shifting from criticism to compassion is the first step in cultivating a healthier relationship with ourselves.

Consider times when you have comforted a friend facing a difficult situation. You likely approached them with empathy and understanding, offering words of encouragement and support. This same approach should be applied to how you treat yourself. Practicing self-compassion involves speaking to yourself gently, acknowledging your struggles without judgment, and giving yourself permission to feel and express emotions. It is about recognizing that everyone makes mistakes and experiences setbacks; these do not define our worth or potential.

Embracing imperfections is another critical aspect of practicing self-compassion. We often strive for perfection, which is an unrealistic standard that sets us up for failure. Instead, viewing our imperfections as opportunities for growth can be transformative. Each imperfection or mistake is a chance to learn and develop resilience. By allowing ourselves to be imperfect, we create space for self-improvement and personal growth. It's important to understand that being human means being flawed, and our value isn't diminished by our weaknesses or failures.

To truly embrace self-compassion, we must also let go of self-blame. Holding onto guilt and continuously blaming ourselves for past actions can prevent us from moving forward. Adopting a mindset of forgiveness is crucial in this process. Forgiveness involves understanding that mistakes are part of the human experience and that they do not negate our intrinsic value. It's about acknowledging our guilt or shame, learning from it, and then releasing it. This does not mean ignoring accountability, but rather approaching our faults with a perspective that fosters healing and growth.

Guidelines for practicing self-forgiveness include:

1. Acknowledge and accept responsibility for your actions without excessive self-criticism.

2. Reflect on the circumstances and context of your mistakes to understand why they happened.

3. Consider what lessons can be learned and how you can avoid similar mistakes in the future.

4. Release the negative emotions associated with the mistake and replace them with constructive thoughts and actions.

Shifting our internal dialogue from one of blame to one of forgiveness allows us to cultivate a more compassionate and loving relationship with ourselves. This shift not only reduces feelings of shame and inadequacy but also promotes emotional well-being and peace.

Offering yourself the same compassion you would offer a friend is an exercise in empathy and understanding. Often, we hold ourselves to higher and harsher standards than we do others. Imagining how we would treat a close friend in a similar situation can help us recalibrate our self-expectations. If a friend were to come to you feeling unworthy or struggling with a mistake, your response would likely be supportive and empathetic. Extend this same response to yourself. Speak encouragingly, remind yourself of your strengths, and validate your feelings without judgment.

Moreover, self-compassion involves recognizing our shared humanity. Everyone faces challenges, makes errors, and deals with insecurities. Understanding that these experiences are universal can alleviate some of the isolation and self-blame we feel. We are not alone in our struggles, and knowing this can foster a sense of connection and belonging.

Transformation through forgiveness is a profound outcome of practicing self-compassion. When we forgive ourselves, we open the door to self-acceptance. Self-acceptance means embracing all parts of ourselves—the good, the bad, and the ugly. It is about recognizing our full, authentic selves and accepting ourselves without conditions. Forgiving yourself paves the way to this acceptance and allows for deeper self-love.

Guidelines for transformation through forgiveness include:

1. Practice self-kindness during moments of failure or difficulty.

2. Engage in self-reflection to identify recurring patterns that hinder self-acceptance.

3. Develop a daily ritual that includes affirmations of self-worth and love.

4. Seek out supportive environments or communities that encourage personal growth.

By integrating these practices into our lives, we begin to reconstruct our self-narratives from ones filled with judgment to ones rich in understanding and love. Self-compassion becomes the foundation upon which self-love and acceptance are built.

Daily Affirmations for Self-Love

Daily affirmations can be a transformative tool in boosting self-love and acceptance. Crafting affirmations that resonate with your personal journey and aspirations is vital. Affirmations are positive statements that reflect who you are or who you want to become. When these statements align with your goals and values, they hold more power. For example, if you are working towards being more confident, an affirmation like "I am confident in my abilities" can reinforce this aim. It is essential to keep these affirmations authentic and specific to your experiences and desires. Personalization encourages a deeper connection and a stronger impact on your mindset.

Gratitude is another powerful tool in shifting focus from self-criticism to self-appreciation. Often, we get caught up in negative self-talk, focusing on our shortcomings rather than acknowledging our strengths. Practicing gratitude helps counteract this tendency. By taking a few moments each day to list things you're grateful for, you begin to recognize the positive aspects of yourself and your life. This shift can significantly improve your overall outlook, making it easier to appreciate and accept yourself as you are. It might feel forced at first, but consistency will lead to more natural feelings of gratitude and self-love.

Affirming your worthiness of love, acceptance, and happiness is crucial in cultivating self-love. Many people struggle with feeling unworthy, which can hinder their ability to experience genuine self-acceptance and joy. Incorporating affirmations that remind you of your inherent worth can help combat these feelings. Statements like "I am deserving of love and respect" or "I embrace happiness and joy in my life" serve as daily reminders of your value. Repeating these affirmations can gradually reshape your beliefs about yourself, promoting a healthier and more loving self-image.

Creating boundaries that protect self-worth and promote self-acceptance is another essential aspect. Boundaries are necessary to maintain your emotional well-being and ensure that your interactions with others are healthy and respectful. They help you define what is acceptable and what is not, ultimately allowing you to safeguard your self-respect and self-love. Establishing boundaries might involve saying no to requests that drain your energy, limiting time spent with negative influences, or standing up for yourself when mistreated. These actions reinforce your worth and help create an environment where self-acceptance can thrive.

To implement these practices effectively, consider setting aside a few minutes each morning or evening dedicated to affirmations. Find a quiet space where you can reflect without distractions. Write down your affirmations or say them aloud, whichever feels more empowering. As you repeat them, try to visualize your affirmations becoming a reality. Picture yourself confidently navigating challenges, appreciating your achievements, and surrounded by positivity. Visualization enhances the emotional connection to your affirmations, making them more impactful.

In addition to affirmations, incorporate a gratitude practice into your daily routine. Keep a journal where you write down three things you're thankful for each day. These could be as simple as a kind gesture from a friend, a moment of peace, or something you appreciate about yourself. Over time, this practice trains your brain to notice and focus on positives, reducing tendencies toward self-criticism.

Affirmations also need periodic review and adjustment. As you grow and your goals evolve, your affirmations should reflect these changes. Regularly assess whether your affirmations still resonate with you and make modifications as needed. This ensures that your practice remains relevant and continues to support your journey towards self-love and acceptance.

When setting boundaries, start by identifying areas in your life where you feel overwhelmed, disrespected, or undervalued. Reflect on these situations and determine what changes are necessary to protect your well-being. Communicate your boundaries clearly and assertively, without feeling guilty. Remember, setting boundaries is an act of self-love and self-preservation. It's about honoring your needs and ensuring that you are treated with the respect you deserve.

For those new to these practices, it might feel uncomfortable or unnatural initially. Persistence is key. The more consistently you engage with your affirmations and gratitude exercises, the more natural they will become. Surround yourself with supportive individuals who encourage your journey towards self-love and acceptance. Being in a positive environment reinforces your efforts and makes the process more enjoyable.

Another helpful tip is to integrate these practices into your existing routines. For instance, recite your affirmations during your morning commute, while brushing your teeth, or before going to bed. This integration makes it easier to maintain consistency without feeling like you're adding extra tasks to your day.

Consider sharing your affirmations with a trusted friend or family member. Having someone else know and support your affirmations can provide additional motivation and accountability. This shared journey can also deepen your relationships, as you both work towards greater self-love and acceptance.

Bringing It All Together

Throughout this chapter, we have explored the importance of practicing self-compassion as a fundamental step toward loving and accepting ourselves unconditionally. By treating ourselves with the same kindness we would offer a dear friend, we can shift from self-criticism to self-nurturance. This practice requires us to be gentle with ourselves, acknowledge our struggles without judgment, and recognize that everyone makes mistakes. Embracing imperfections allows us to grow and learn rather than feel defeated by our flaws. Letting go of self-blame and adopting forgiveness can lead to profound self-acceptance and emotional well-being.

We've also discussed incorporating daily affirmations and gratitude practices into our lives to reinforce self-love. Personalizing affirmations ensure they resonate deeply with our individual journeys, while gratitude helps shift focus from negative self-talk to positive self-appreciation. Additionally, setting boundaries protects our self-worth and promotes healthier interactions. These practices are not always easy at first but become more natural with consistency and support. Through patience and dedication, we can transform our inner dialogue and cultivate a compassionate relationship with ourselves.

Chapter Four

Mindfulness and Presence

M indfulness and presence are practices that bring us into the now, enriching our lives with clarity and peace. Living in the moment allows us to experience life more fully and reduce the overwhelming stress that often stems from dwelling on the past or worrying about the future. By embracing mindfulness, we embark on a journey toward heightened awareness, which helps us manage our thoughts and emotions more effectively. This practice enables us to reconnect with our inner selves and find solace amidst the turbulence of our daily routines.

In this chapter, we will explore the essentials of mindfulness practice, including techniques such as mindful breathing exercises and body scan meditation, which guide us in anchoring our attention to the present moment. We'll also discuss how incorporating these methods into our daily lives can foster a sense of inner tranquility and balance. The chapter will delve into practical strategies for developing a non-reactive and compassionate mindset, highlighting the importance of observing thoughts without judgment and cultivating resilience. As you read on, you'll discover ways to integrate mindfulness seamlessly into everyday activities, transforming ordinary moments into opportunities for profound self-awareness and peace.

The Essentials of Mindfulness Practice

Understanding the foundational principles of mindfulness is paramount for cultivating presence and achieving inner peace. Mindfulness, at its core, is the practice of being fully aware and present in the moment. It involves paying attention to our thoughts, feelings, and surroundings without judgment or distraction. This heightened state of awareness can significantly reduce stress, promote mental clarity, and enhance overall well-being.

Being present plays a crucial role in our daily lives by promoting awareness and reducing stress. In our fast-paced world, we often find ourselves caught up in a whirlwind of activities and responsibilities, leaving little time to pause and reflect. This constant state of busyness can lead to heightened stress levels and burnout. However, by incorporating mindfulness into our routine, we can create moments of stillness and tranquility. These moments allow us to reconnect with ourselves and our surroundings, fostering a sense of calm and balance.

One of the most accessible ways to practice being in the "here and now" is through mindful breathing exercises. By focusing on our breath, we anchor ourselves in the present moment, making it easier to let go of distracting thoughts. A simple technique involves taking slow, deep breaths, inhaling through the nose, and exhaling through the mouth. As we breathe, we can pay attention to the sensation of the air entering and leaving our body. This practice not only helps center our mind but also promotes relaxation and reduces anxiety.

Another effective mindfulness technique is the body scan meditation. This practice involves mentally scanning the body from head to toe, paying attention to any sensations or areas of tension. By bringing awareness to different parts of the body, we can release physical stress and cultivate a deeper connection with ourselves. The body scan meditation can be particularly beneficial before bedtime, helping to calm the mind and prepare for restful sleep.

Developing a mindful attitude is essential for noticing sensations, emotions, and thoughts without reactivity. Often, we react automatically to our thoughts and feelings, leading to emotional upheaval and impulsive actions. Mindfulness encourages us to observe our internal experiences without judgment or attachment. For instance, if we notice a feeling of anger arising, instead of immediately reacting, we can acknowledge the emotion and explore its underlying cause. This non-reactive awareness fosters resilience and emotional stability, allowing us to respond to situations more thoughtfully.

Integrating mindfulness into daily routines can enhance our overall well-being and inner peace. There are numerous opportunities throughout the day to practice mindfulness, whether it's during morning coffee, while commuting, or even while doing household chores. For example, when washing the dishes, we can focus on the sensation of the water on our hands, the smell of the soap, and the sound of the running tap. By being fully present in these seemingly mundane activities, we transform them into moments of mindfulness, enriching our experience of everyday life.

Guidelines for practicing mindfulness can further aid in this journey. It's helpful to set aside dedicated time each day, even if it's just a few minutes, to engage in mindfulness practices. Consistency is key, as regular practice reinforces the habit of mindfulness. Additionally, creating a peaceful environment free from distractions can enhance the experience. Whether it's a quiet room, a cozy corner, or a serene outdoor space, having a designated area for mindfulness can make it easier to focus and relax.

Observing our thoughts without attachment or judgment is another important aspect of mindfulness. Our minds are constantly generating thoughts, many of which can be negative or unproductive. Instead of getting entangled in these thoughts, mindfulness teaches us to view them as passing clouds in the sky. We acknowledge their presence but do not let them define our reality. This perspective shift allows us to maintain a sense of inner peace, even amidst mental chatter.

Noticing sensations, emotions, and thoughts without reactivity is closely linked to practicing non-judgmental awareness in all experiences. Life is full of challenges and uncertainties, and it's natural to encounter difficult emotions. Mindfulness encourages us to embrace these experiences without labeling them as good or bad. By accepting our emotions as they are, we develop a compassionate relationship with ourselves. This self-compassion not only nurtures inner peace but also enhances our capacity to empathize with others.

Building resilience through a mindful attitude is integral to navigating life's ups and downs. Resilience is the ability to bounce back from adversity, and mindfulness equips us with the tools to do so. When faced with challenges, a mindful approach allows us to remain grounded and centered. Rather than being overwhelmed by difficulties, we learn to approach them with curiosity and openness. This resilient mindset empowers us to adapt and grow, fostering a profound sense of inner strength.

Implementing Meditation and Grounding Techniques

Living in the moment can be a powerful tool for achieving inner peace, especially when armed with practical tools that enhance mindfulness and mental clarity. Let's delve into several approaches that can help you stay rooted amidst daily challenges.

To begin, it's beneficial to understand the various types of meditation. Each style offers unique advantages and can be tailored to meet your specific needs. Mindfulness meditation, for example, focuses on maintaining a non-judgmental awareness of the present moment. This practice involves paying attention to your breath, thoughts, and sensations as they arise, without getting entangled in them. By regularly engaging in mindfulness meditation, you become more attuned to what's happening right now, which can significantly reduce feelings of stress and anxiety.

Similarly, loving-kindness meditation encourages positive emotional states by fostering a sense of compassion and acceptance toward yourself and others. During this meditation, you silently repeat phrases such as "May I be happy," "May I be healthy," and "May I live with ease." This practice is particularly effective for individuals dealing with emotional wounds or loss, as it helps cultivate an attitude of kindness and warmth, promoting emotional healing over time.

Guided visualizations are another form of meditation that can greatly enhance relaxation and focus. In these sessions, a guide leads you through a series of mental images designed to bring about a state of calm and concentration. Picture yourself walking through a serene forest or standing by a peaceful ocean. These vivid visualizations can transport your mind away from stressors, offering a temporary respite and a chance to recharge mentally and emotionally.

Understanding the neurological and physiological benefits of these practices further underscores their importance. Meditation has been shown to reduce cortisol levels, the hormone associated with stress. Regular practice can also enhance cognitive function, improving your ability to focus, concentrate, and process information more effectively. When you understand how these techniques influence your brain and body, it becomes easier to commit to making them a regular part of your routine.

Grounding exercises offer tangible ways to stabilize yourself during moments of distress. One effective method is the five-senses grounding technique. When you're feeling overwhelmed, take a moment to identify something you can see, hear, touch, smell, and taste. Focusing on these sensory details can quickly bring you back to the present moment, diverting your mind from anxious thoughts and grounding you in reality.

Visualization can also serve as an excellent grounding tool. Imagine roots growing from the soles of your feet deep into the earth, anchoring you firmly. This mental image can create a profound sense of stability, helping you regain your footing when life's challenges threaten to sweep you away.

Integrating these grounding practices into daily routines can have lasting benefits for emotional regulation. For instance, start your day with a brief mindfulness meditation session to set a calm tone, and use the five-senses grounding technique whenever you feel stress creeping in. Over time, these practices become second nature, arming you with tools to navigate emotional turbulence with greater ease.

Emotional regulation is crucial for sustained peace. By regularly practicing meditation and grounding exercises, you build resilience and learn to respond rather than react to emotional triggers. This shift not only promotes inner peace but also enhances your interactions with others, making relationships more harmonious.

Final Thoughts

Living in the moment is a powerful way to enhance inner peace and overall well-being. This chapter has explored various mindfulness practices, including mindful breathing, body scan meditation, and grounding exercises, all aimed at fostering a deeper connection with ourselves and our surroundings. By paying attention to our thoughts, emotions, and sensations without judgment, we create space for calm and clarity in our daily lives. These techniques help us remain present, reducing stress and promoting emotional stability.

As you integrate these practices into your routine, remember that consistency is key. Finding small moments throughout the day to engage in mindfulness can transform ordinary activities into opportunities for presence and tranquility. Whether it's during your morning coffee or while commuting, being fully present enriches your experience of life, nurturing a sense of inner peace. Embracing this mindful approach allows you to navigate challenges with resilience and compassion, ultimately leading to a more balanced and harmonious existence.

Chapter Five

Navigating Emotional Turmoil

Navigating emotional turmoil involves finding ways to manage intense feelings and achieve a sense of balance in our lives. Emotions are often powerful, sometimes overwhelming forces that can steer us off course if we do not understand them. By recognizing emotions not as enemies but as guides, we can begin the journey of turning turmoil into tranquility. Emotional awareness helps us see these feelings for what they are: indicators of deeper issues or needs. Instead of reacting impulsively, we can learn to navigate through life's challenges with greater clarity and purpose.

This chapter delves into understanding the nature of emotions and how they can serve as valuable signposts in our internal landscape. You will discover techniques for regulating your emotions, from mindful breathing and self-soothing techniques to grounding exercises and movement therapy. Embracing emotions without judgment and developing emotional intelligence will also be key components discussed, helping you build stronger relationships and improve your overall well-being. By the end of this chapter, you will have practical tools to manage intense emotions and find a balanced approach to handling life's emotional ups and downs.

Understanding the Nature of Emotions

Emotional awareness is fundamental in balancing intense feelings and managing emotional turmoil. Emotions, often seen as disruptive forces, can serve as valuable signposts. These indicators provide a glimpse into our inner state, guiding us toward understanding and self-regulation. To navigate through life's challenges, one must become attuned to these emotional signposts.

Imagine emotions as signals on a map. Just as a traveler relies on signs to reach a destination, we rely on our emotions to understand where we are internally. For instance, anger might indicate that a boundary has been violated, while sadness could signal a need for connection or healing. By recognizing these signposts, we can begin to address the underlying causes rather than merely reacting to the surface-level feelings.

Moreover, each emotion carries invaluable messages that contribute to personal growth and healing. Anger is not just a flare of temper; it is a call to action against perceived injustice or mistreatment. Similarly, fear often highlights areas where we feel insecure or unprepared. By tuning into these messages, we gain insights into our needs and vulnerabilities. This recognition is the first step toward transforming these feelings into opportunities for improvement and healing.

For example, consider how sadness brings about reflection. It urges us to slow down and assess what we might have lost or what could be missing from our lives. Rather than dismissing this feeling as merely unpleasant, acknowledging its message can lead to profound personal insights. When we allow ourselves to dive deeper into what our emotions are communicating, we begin to uncover layers of our identity that were previously hidden.

Embracing emotions without judgment is another crucial aspect of emotional awareness. Often, we criticize ourselves for feeling a certain way, labeling emotions as "good" or "bad." This binary approach can hinder true emotional processing and acceptance. Instead, viewing emotions as natural responses devoid of positive or negative labels fosters an environment of self-acceptance and discovery.

Think of this process as welcoming a friend who visits unexpectedly. Even if the visit disrupts your routine, you do not judge them for showing up. You simply acknowledge their presence and engage with them. Similarly, by welcoming emotions as they arise—without immediate judgment—we create space for understanding and learning. This acceptance allows us to process and eventually release these feelings constructively.

Developing emotional intelligence is vital for navigating complex feelings with clarity and empathy. Emotional intelligence involves the ability to recognize, understand, manage, and harness emotions effectively. It is not just about knowing what we feel, but also comprehending why we feel that way and how to respond appropriately.

A practical example of emotional intelligence is during interpersonal conflicts. Someone with high emotional intelligence can sense their own rising frustration and choose to address it calmly rather than lashing out. They can express their feelings in a way that fosters mutual understanding rather than escalating the conflict. This skill builds stronger relationships and promotes a healthier emotional landscape.

Consider a time when you felt overwhelmed by a situation. Perhaps you reacted impulsively, only to regret it later.

Developing emotional intelligence helps mitigate such instances. By pausing and reflecting on your emotions before acting, you can choose responses that align more closely with your values and goals. This discipline enhances both personal well-being and interpersonal connections.

Incorporating emotional intelligence into daily life requires continuous practice and mindfulness. Simple exercises like journaling emotions, practicing empathy by putting oneself in others' shoes, and seeking feedback on emotional reactions can significantly bolster one's emotional intelligence over time. This ongoing effort will yield dividends in terms of improved emotional regulation and healthier interactions.

In summary, exploring the significance of emotional awareness in balancing intense feelings involves several key components. First, recognizing emotions as signposts that guide us toward deeper understanding and self-regulation. Second, tuning into the messages each emotion carries, which provides valuable cues for personal growth and healing. Third, acknowledging emotions without judgment, which fosters acceptance and self-discovery. Fourth, developing emotional intelligence to navigate complex feelings with clarity and empathy.

Techniques for Emotional Regulation

Breathing Techniques: Utilizing mindful breathing exercises to anchor oneself during emotional upheavals is a cornerstone of managing intense emotions. Breathing is something we often take for granted, but it is a powerful tool that can be harnessed to bring about calm and focus. When emotions run high, our breathing tends to become shallow and rapid, exacerbating the feeling of panic or distress. Mindful breathing involves taking slow, deep breaths, focusing on the rhythm and sensation of each breath. This practice helps slow down the heart rate and brings the mind back to the present moment.

One simple yet effective method is the Box Breathing Method. This technique involves inhaling slowly for four counts, holding the breath for four counts, exhaling for four counts, and then pausing for another count of four before repeating the cycle. Box breathing not only soothes the nervous system but also provides a structured way to regain control over one's emotional state. Practicing this regularly can make it easier to utilize during moments of intense emotion.

Self-Regulation Strategies: Another practical strategy for managing intense emotions is self-regulation through self-soothing techniques. These methods aim to help individuals calm themselves during times of emotional stress. One effective approach is progressive muscle relaxation. This technique involves tensing and then slowly relaxing different muscle groups in the body. By focusing on the physical sensations associated with tension and relaxation, individuals can divert their attention from their emotional turmoil and foster a sense of inner peace.

Progressive muscle relaxation can be combined with breathing exercises for enhanced effect. For instance, as you inhale, tense a specific muscle group (like your shoulders), hold the tension for a few seconds, and then release the tension while exhaling. Moving through various muscle groups—from your feet up to your head—can result in a comprehensive sense of relaxation.

Emotional release journaling is another valuable self-regulation strategy. Writing down your thoughts and feelings provides an outlet for emotions that might otherwise remain bottled up. Journaling can serve as a reflective practice, helping you identify triggers, patterns, and potential solutions to your emotional challenges. Regularly setting aside time to journal can deepen your self-awareness and improve your ability to manage intense emotions.

Movement Therapy: Engaging in physical activities like yoga or dance can be incredibly beneficial for releasing pent-up emotions and restoring emotional equilibrium. Movement therapy allows the body to naturally release stress and tension, promoting overall well-being. Physical activity increases the production of endorphins, the body's natural mood lifters, which can significantly improve emotional health.

Yoga, with its combination of physical postures, breathing exercises, and meditation, offers a holistic approach to managing emotions. Each pose targets different muscle groups and energy centers in the body, aiding in the release of physical and emotional tension. The mindfulness aspect of yoga encourages individuals to stay present, grounding them in their bodies and reducing anxiety and stress.

Dance, on the other hand, provides a more dynamic form of movement therapy. It allows for creative expression, letting individuals physically manifest their emotions. Dancing to music can be both cathartic and joyous, offering a unique avenue to process and release emotions. Whether it is an organized dance class or simply dancing in your living room, movement therapy through dance can be an enjoyable and effective means of emotional regulation.

Grounding Exercises: Grounding exercises are essential for centering oneself amidst emotional turmoil. These techniques involve connecting deeply with the present moment through sensory experiences, which can help distract from overwhelming emotions and bring a sense of stability. One common grounding exercise is the Five Senses Check-In. This involves identifying five things you can see, four things you can touch, three things you can hear, two things you can smell, and one thing you can taste. By engaging all five senses, this exercise helps root you firmly in the present, providing immediate relief from emotional overwhelm.

Barefoot grounding, also known as earthing, is another effective grounding technique. Walking barefoot on natural surfaces like grass, sand, or soil can have a soothing effect on the mind and body. The physical connection with the earth is believed to balance the body's electrical charge, leading to reduced stress and improved emotional health. Spending even a few minutes walking barefoot outdoors can promote a sense of calm and centeredness.

Summary and Reflections

Navigating intense emotions and finding balance is a continuous journey that requires mindful attention and practice. Understanding that emotions serve as signposts rather than obstacles can transform the way we engage with our feelings. By acknowledging the messages behind our emotions, whether they signal a need for connection, healing, or action, we open the door to deeper self-awareness and personal growth. Embracing these emotions without judgment further fosters an environment of acceptance and discovery, allowing us to process and release them constructively.

Developing skills such as emotional intelligence and employing techniques like mindful breathing, self-soothing, movement therapy, and grounding exercises are essential tools in this journey. They help us manage our responses effectively, build stronger relationships, and maintain a healthier emotional landscape. As you continue to explore these strategies, remember that this journey is unique to you. With patience and practice, you will find the balance and peace needed to navigate life's emotional ups and downs.

Chapter Six

The Power of Intention and Affirmation

Harnessing the mind's power to shape reality through intention and affirmation begins with understanding the significance of these practices. By deliberately focusing our thoughts and expressing them as affirmations, we can influence our mindset and actions in profound ways. This chapter delves into how meaningful affirmations can transform our inner landscape by aligning with our deepest goals and desires.

Throughout the chapter, readers will explore methods to create effective, personalized affirmations that resonate on a deep level. The importance of language, particularly the use of the present tense, will be examined to understand how it shapes our subconscious beliefs. Additionally, the chapter will offer practical strategies for integrating affirmations into daily routines, ensuring they remain a powerful tool for personal growth. By the end, readers will be equipped with the knowledge to use affirmations and intentions as a compass guiding them toward their aspirations.

Creating Meaningful Affirmations

Affirmations, when crafted and used effectively, can profoundly transform one's mindset and actions. The process begins with developing affirmations that resonate deeply with individual goals and desires. This initial step is crucial because the more personal and meaningful an affirmation is, the more potent it becomes in influencing one's thoughts and behaviors.

To craft personal affirmations, start by identifying your core values, aspirations, and areas where you seek improvement or change. Imagine a scenario where someone aims to develop self-confidence. An effective affirmation might be, "I am confident in my abilities and trust myself to succeed." This statement directly addresses the individual's goal of boosting self-assurance and is imbued with positive reinforcement.

Furthermore, it's essential to ensure these affirmations are stated in the present tense, as if the desired outcome is already a reality. This linguistic technique helps convince the subconscious mind that what is being affirmed is true, fostering a mindset of abundance and possibility. For instance, instead of saying, "I will be confident," say, "I am confident." This subtle shift can create a significant difference in how your mind processes the affirmation.

Once the affirmations are crafted, they should be personalized to empower individuals to focus on specific areas for growth and manifestation. Personalized affirmations serve as a mental compass, guiding attention toward the desired aspects of life. When a person consistently focuses on affirmations related to specific goals, it reinforces their commitment and dedication to achieving those goals. This practice not only helps maintain clarity but also strengthens resolve, making it easier to overcome obstacles that may arise along the way.

A critical aspect of personalized affirmations is tailoring them to address personal challenges. Each individual faces unique circumstances and hurdles that can affect their journey toward self-improvement. By customizing affirmations to reflect these challenges, one can enhance their effectiveness. For example, if someone struggles with anxiety, an affirmation like, "I am calm, centered, and in control," can help reduce stress and promote a sense of peace. Tailoring affirmations in this manner ensures they are relevant and directly applicable to the person's life, thereby increasing their impact.

Moreover, incorporating sensory details and emotional elements can further amplify the power of affirmations. Instead of a simple statement, adding vivid imagery and feelings can make the affirmation more compelling. Imagine someone wanting to improve their public speaking skills; they might use an affirmation like, "I feel energized and articulate when I speak to an audience, engaging them with confidence and poise." This not only affirms the desired outcome but also evokes the emotions and sensations associated with successful public speaking, making the affirmation more effective.

The repetition of affirmations plays a pivotal role in rewiring the subconscious mind for lasting change. Consistently repeating affirmations embeds them into the subconscious, gradually altering deep-seated beliefs and thought patterns. For instance, someone seeking to develop a healthier lifestyle might repeat, "I am committed to nourishing my body with healthy foods and regular exercise." Over time, this repeated affirmation can shift deeply ingrained habits and promote healthier choices naturally.

To maximize the benefits, it's advisable to integrate affirmation practices into daily routines. One could begin the day by reciting affirmations aloud, writing them down in a journal, or even placing them on sticky notes around the house. These small but consistent actions reinforce the affirmations and keep them at the forefront of one's mind.

It's also beneficial to adopt a reflective approach, periodically assessing the impact of the affirmations and making adjustments as needed. Life is dynamic, and so are our goals and challenges. Regularly reflecting on the efficacy of affirmations ensures they continue to align with current needs and aspirations. It's a process of ongoing refinement, much like adjusting the sails of a ship to stay on course.

To illustrate, consider someone who initially uses an affirmation focused on career advancement, such as, "I am successful and valued in my profession." Over time, as they achieve their career goals, they might shift their focus toward personal relationships, crafting a new affirmation like, "I am surrounded by loving and supportive friends and family." This adaptability ensures that the individual's affirmations remain pertinent and powerful throughout different stages of life.

The Science Behind Intention Setting and Visualization

Understanding the psychological and neuroscientific principles behind setting intentions and visualization techniques can profoundly impact personal growth and transformation. At the core of these practices lies the concept of neuroplasticity, the brain's remarkable ability to reorganize itself by forming new neural connections throughout life. This adaptability is crucial for intention setting and visualization because it demonstrates that our thoughts and focus can actively shape our brain's structure and function.

Neuroplasticity and Intention

When we set clear intentions, we essentially direct our mental energy toward a specific goal or outcome. This deliberate focus enables the brain to prioritize certain neural pathways over others, gradually strengthening those associated with our intentions. For example, if an individual consistently focuses on becoming more confident, their brain will start to rewire itself to support this intention by reinforcing pathways linked to self-assurance and diminishing those tied to self-doubt. The more frequently one engages in this intentional focus, the more ingrained these positive changes become, leading to lasting shifts in thought patterns and behaviors.

One key aspect of neuroplasticity is its reliance on repetition. Consistent intention setting acts as a powerful tool for harnessing the mind's power to shape reality. Each time an individual consciously focuses on their intentions, they are essentially rehearsing their desired outcome, making it easier for the brain to adapt and incorporate these changes into their everyday life. Over time, this consistent practice can lead to significant transformations, both mentally and emotionally, as the brain becomes more attuned to the individual's goals and aspirations.

Visualization as a Manifestation Tool

Another potent technique for leveraging the brain's neuroplasticity is visualization. Visualization involves creating detailed mental images of desired outcomes, allowing individuals to experience their goals in their mind's eye before they materialize in reality. This practice not only enhances motivation but also strengthens the belief in one's ability to achieve these goals.

When individuals visualize their objectives with vivid detail, they engage multiple areas of the brain, including those responsible for motor control, memory, and sensory perception. This multisensory engagement helps to create a more profound and realistic mental experience, making it easier for the brain to process and internalize these visualizations as genuine possibilities. As a result, individuals who regularly practice visualization are more likely to stay motivated, focused, and committed to their goals, as their brains have already begun to prepare for success.

Moreover, visualization can serve as a rehearsal for real-life situations, helping individuals build confidence and reduce anxiety. For instance, someone preparing for a public speaking event might visualize themselves delivering a successful speech, picturing the audience's positive reactions and feeling the sense of accomplishment that comes with it. By repeatedly practicing this mental scenario, the individual can reduce nervousness and enhance their performance when the actual event takes place.

Combining Intention Setting and Visualization

While intention setting and visualization are powerful tools on their own, their combined effect can be even more transformative. By setting clear, specific intentions and regularly visualizing the achievement of these goals, individuals can create a robust mental framework that supports their aspirations. This combination helps reinforce the brain's neural pathways associated with the desired outcome, making it easier to stay focused and motivated in pursuing one's dreams.

To maximize the benefits of these practices, it's essential to approach them with consistency and clarity. Individuals should take the time to articulate their intentions clearly, ensuring that they align with their core values and long-term goals. Once these intentions are set, regular visualization sessions can help keep the mind engaged and focused, providing the mental rehearsal needed to turn these aspirations into reality.

Additionally, it's important to remember that progress may not always be linear. There may be setbacks and challenges along the way, but maintaining a consistent practice of intention setting and visualization can help individuals stay resilient and adaptable. By continually reinforcing these positive neural pathways, the brain becomes better equipped to navigate obstacles and remain committed to the ultimate goal.

Practical Applications and Techniques

To effectively incorporate intention setting and visualization into daily life, individuals can follow a few practical steps. First, it's helpful to establish a routine that includes dedicated time for these practices. This could be as simple as spending a few minutes each morning and evening reflecting on one's intentions and visualizing their achievement. Consistency is key, as regular practice helps reinforce the desired neural changes.

During these sessions, it can be beneficial to use tools such as journaling or vision boards. Writing down intentions and visualizing goals through images and words can create a tangible connection to one's aspirations, making them feel more achievable and real. Moreover, these tools can serve as reminders of one's commitments, helping to maintain focus and motivation throughout the day.

Another effective technique is guided visualization, where individuals listen to audio recordings that lead them through a structured visualization process. These guided sessions can provide additional support and inspiration, helping individuals to explore their goals in greater depth and detail. By incorporating these various methods, individuals can create a comprehensive approach to intention setting and visualization, maximizing their potential for personal growth and transformation.

Final Thoughts

Harnessing the mind's power to shape reality is a journey of inner transformation, grounded in the creation and repetition of personalized affirmations. By focusing on positive, present-tense statements that resonate deeply with our core values and aspirations, we direct our mental energy toward specific goals. This practice helps to rewire our subconscious mind, gradually shifting our thoughts and behaviors toward a more empowered and confident self. The integration of sensory details and emotional elements further enhances the impact of these affirmations, making them vivid and compelling.

To solidify these changes, it's crucial to incorporate affirmations into our daily routines and remain adaptable as our goals evolve. Regularly reassessing and adjusting affirmations ensures they continue to align with our current needs and aspirations. Combining this practice with visualization techniques creates a powerful synergy, reinforcing our intentions and helping us stay focused and motivated. This dynamic approach fosters resilience, guiding us through challenges and supporting our journey toward personal growth and transformation.

Chapter Seven

Connecting With Inner Wisdom

Connecting with inner wisdom involves a delicate balance between understanding the ego's voice and listening to our intuitive guidance. Many people find themselves caught in the conflict between these two internal voices, often swayed by the louder, more insistent demands of the ego. The ego thrives on fear, judgment, and the need for validation from external sources, which can obscure the softer yet profound insights of intuition. By recognizing the influence of the ego, we can learn to quiet its noise and create space for deeper, more authentic wisdom to emerge.

This chapter delves into distinguishing the ego from intuition, offering practical approaches to identify when the ego is at play and how it can overshadow our inner guidance. We will explore various ways in which fears and insecurities cloud our intuition, making it difficult to trust our inner voice. Through understanding and awareness, we can begin to unveil intuitive signals that often come with clarity and peace rather than anxiety and doubt. Additionally, the chapter will provide methods to discern true intuitive guidance from external influences, paving the way for a more harmonious connection with our inner selves.

Difference Between Ego and Intuition

In our journey toward connecting with inner wisdom, it is essential to understand the distinction between the ego's voice and intuitive guidance. These two voices often compete for our attention but come from vastly different places within us. The ego, primarily rooted in fear and limitation, tends to focus on self-preservation and external validation. Recognizing its influence can help us become more attuned to genuine intuitive insights that stem from a place of clarity and peace.

Recognizing the Ego's Influence

The ego operates from a space of fear and limitation. It is the part of us that constantly seeks approval and validation from the outside world. This voice is loud and persistent, often creating an endless loop of worry and doubt. It thrives on comparisons, leading us to measure our worth against others. For example, when considering a new job offer, the ego might focus on potential failures or how others will perceive us rather than on what is truly best for our growth and happiness.

Understanding How Fears and Insecurities Can Cloud Intuitive Messages

Our fears and insecurities often act as barriers, clouding our ability to receive clear intuitive messages. When we are consumed by what-ifs and worst-case scenarios, our ability to tap into deeper wisdom becomes significantly impaired. For instance, someone who has experienced repeated rejection may find it difficult to trust their intuition when entering new relationships. The fear of getting hurt again overshadows the quiet, assuring voice that comes from within. By acknowledging these fears, we begin to clear the path for our intuition to emerge more clearly.

Unveiling Intuitive Signals

Intuitive insights, in contrast, come with a sense of clarity and peace. Unlike the ego's noisy chatter, intuition speaks softly but profoundly. It feels like a gentle nudge in the right direction. You might experience this during a moment of calm, such as taking a walk in nature or relaxing in a warm bath. In these moments, intuitive guidance can appear as a sudden realization or a subtle feeling of knowing the right thing to do.

Learning to Discern Intuitive Guidance from External Influences

One challenge in connecting with inner wisdom is learning to distinguish between intuitive guidance and external influences. In today's world, we are bombarded with opinions and advice from various sources, including friends, family, social media, and society at large. These external voices can sometimes overshadow our internal guidance. On the other hand, Intuition does not shout; it whispers. It often comes in the form of a gut feeling, a sudden insight, or a quiet sense of certainty. Paying attention to these subtle signals can guide us to make decisions that are in alignment with our true selves. To discern the difference, it helps to reflect on how you feel when receiving a message. True intuitive guidance leaves you feeling aligned and at peace, while external influences often leave you feeling more confused or anxious.

Recognizing the Ego's Influence

It is crucial to recognize patterns of self-doubt and criticism originating from the ego. These patterns often manifest as negative self-talk, telling us we are not good enough, smart enough, or deserving enough. By becoming aware of these patterns, we can start to question their validity and lessen their power over us. For example, when preparing for a presentation, the ego might bombard you with thoughts of inadequacy. However, recognizing this as the ego's voice allows you to shift your focus back to your preparation and the value you bring to your audience.

Understanding How Fears and Insecurities Can Cloud Intuitive Messages

Cultivating awareness of how fears and insecurities manifest can significantly enhance our connection with inner wisdom. These feelings often originate from past experiences where we felt vulnerable or hurt. They create a fog that obscures our intuitive signals. By identifying these fears, we can work through them and reduce their impact. For example, journaling about past experiences and how they have shaped current fears can be a powerful way to gain clarity and release these emotional blockages.

Exercises for Enhancing and Trusting Your Inner Guidance

In our journey toward connecting with inner wisdom, engaging in meditative practices is paramount. Meditation quiets the mind and enhances receptivity to intuitive messages. It allows us to step away from the noise of daily life and create a still space within ourselves where deeper insights can surface. When we meditate, we focus on our breath, allowing thoughts to pass without attachment. This practice not only calms the mind but also opens channels to intuition, fostering a clearer connection with our inner voice.

Using focused breathing techniques to center the mind and open these channels can significantly aid in this process. Begin by sitting comfortably, closing your eyes, and taking deep, slow breaths. Inhale fully, allowing your lungs to expand, then exhale completely, letting go of any tension. As you continue this practice, notice how your thoughts begin to settle, creating a serene environment conducive to receiving intuitive guidance. Regular meditation, even for a few minutes each day, helps cultivate this sense of inner stillness and enhances your ability to tune into your intuition.

Embracing stillness and silence as pathways to heightened intuition is another effective approach. In our busy lives, finding moments of complete silence can be challenging, yet it is in these quiet moments that our inner voice becomes most audible. By intentionally carving out time for solitude and silence, we create a sacred space where our inner guidance can emerge. This practice does not necessarily require long periods; even brief moments of quiet contemplation can lead to profound intuitive insights.

Creative expression serves as a powerful tool to tap into intuitive insights. Engaging in activities such as journaling, painting, or making music allows us to access a different part of our consciousness where intuition often resides. When we immerse ourselves in creative pursuits, we enter a state of flow—a mental state where we are fully present and engaged in the activity at hand. This state of flow bypasses the logical mind and connects us directly to our intuitive wisdom.

Allowing creative expression to serve as a conduit for intuitive messages to surface can be transformative. For instance, journaling provides a structured way to explore thoughts and feelings, uncovering underlying intuitive impressions. Similarly, painting or playing music can facilitate a spontaneous release of emotions and insights that might remain hidden otherwise. By dedicating time to creative outlets, we enable our inner voice to speak through artistic expressions, revealing valuable guidance and understanding.

Exploring the power of creative outlets in channeling inner guidance also emphasizes the importance of trusting the process. Often, we may hesitate to engage in creative activities due to self-doubt or fear of judgment. However, it is crucial to recognize that creativity is not about perfection but about authentic self-expression. Embrace the vulnerability that comes with creative endeavors, knowing that each stroke of the brush or written word brings you closer to your true self and deeper intuitive knowledge.

Embracing vulnerability is an essential aspect of trusting one's inner guidance. Trusting intuition requires courage, as it often involves stepping into the unknown and defying conventional logic. Acknowledging and accepting our fears and insecurities is the first step toward overcoming them. When we recognize that vulnerability is not a weakness but a pathway to authentic self-expression, we can more readily follow our intuitive insights without fear of judgment or failure.

Overcoming the fear of judgment or failure in following intuitive insights empowers us to live more authentically. Society often conditions us to prioritize rational thinking over intuitive knowing, leading to a disconnect from our inner wisdom. By embracing vulnerability, we allow ourselves to break free from these constraints and honor our intuitive guidance. This shift in mindset fosters a sense of curiosity and openness toward intuitive experiences, further strengthening our connection to inner wisdom.

Cultivating a mindset of curiosity and openness toward intuitive guidance involves viewing each intuitive message as an opportunity for growth. Rather than dismissing intuitive nudges, approach them with a sense of wonder and eagerness to learn. This attitude not only reinforces trust in your intuition but also encourages continuous exploration of your inner landscape. By maintaining an open and curious mindset, you create an environment where intuitive insights can flourish and guide you toward greater self-awareness and fulfillment.

Reflective practices play a significant role in deepening trust in intuitive messages. Self-reflection offers a means to examine our experiences and recognize patterns or insights that arise from within. Through reflective practices, we can discern between fleeting thoughts and genuine intuitive guidance, honing our ability to distinguish the latter with greater accuracy.

One simple yet effective reflective practice is journaling. Documenting your thoughts, emotions, and intuitive impressions can provide clarity and reinforce trust in your inner wisdom. Regularly reviewing your journal entries allows you to observe recurring themes or messages, validating the authenticity of your intuitive guidance. Additionally, engaging in reflective questioning—such as asking yourself why certain intuitions arise or how they align with your values—can deepen your understanding and trust in your inner voice.

Another reflective practice is meditation combined with contemplation. After a meditative session, spend a few moments contemplating any intuitive messages or feelings that surfaced. Reflect on their possible meanings and relevance to your current situation. This practice bridges the gap between meditation and everyday life, integrating intuitive insights into your conscious awareness.

Ultimately, incorporating these practices into your daily routine fosters a strong connection with your inner wisdom. By engaging in meditative practices, embracing creative expression, honoring vulnerability, and committing to reflective practices, you amplify your intuitive abilities and cultivate unwavering trust in your intuitive knowing. This journey toward deeper self-understanding and spiritual healing is a transformative process that empowers you to navigate life's challenges with confidence and clarity.

Final Thoughts

Throughout this chapter, we have explored the vital distinction between the ego's voice and intuitive guidance. The ego, driven by fear and external validation, often clouds our true inner wisdom with self-doubt and criticism. By recognizing these patterns and understanding how fears and insecurities can obstruct our intuition, we begin to clear a path toward deeper self-awareness.

Embracing moments of stillness allows us to hear the soft yet profound whispers of our intuition, guiding us with clarity and peace.

Connecting with our inner voice involves discerning genuine intuitive insights from external influences. This requires reflection and an openness to feelings of alignment and resonance that accompany true guidance. By practicing creative expression, meditation, and reflective exercises, we enhance our ability to tune into this inner wisdom. Trusting our intuition means embracing vulnerability and viewing each intuitive message as a valuable opportunity for growth and self-discovery. As we journey forward, fostering trust in our intuition will empower us to navigate life's challenges with greater confidence and authenticity.

Chapter Eight

Living Authentically

Living authentically involves embracing and honoring your unique traits. It is about recognizing and celebrating individuality in a world that often pressures us to conform. Each person has distinct qualities that make them who they are, and these qualities deserve recognition and respect. By acknowledging these aspects of yourself, you gain a clearer picture of who you truly are. This process not only highlights the diversity of human experience but also underscores the richness it brings to life.

In this chapter, we will explore how self-awareness and self-acceptance are key to living authentically. We will discuss practical strategies for setting personal boundaries that safeguard your sense of self and for creating an environment where your true self can thrive. You will learn the importance of cultivating self-compassion and trusting your intuition for more fulfilling decision-making. Additionally, we will reflect on core values as guiding principles that align your actions with who you are at your core. Through these discussions, you will find ways to navigate societal expectations while making decisions based on your inner truths and values.

Acknowledging and Embracing Authenticity

Embracing your individuality is a powerful journey that celebrates the essence of who you are. Understanding your own qualities starts with being aware of yourself."'

Recognizing and celebrating your distinct qualities fosters self-acceptance. When you accept yourself as you are, you create a solid foundation for personal growth and development. This self-acceptance is not about becoming complacent or ignoring areas where improvement is needed. Instead, it is about acknowledging that you are a work in progress and that your uniqueness is something to be valued.

Self-acceptance also involves letting go of negative self-judgment and critical thoughts. Many people struggle with an inner critic that constantly points out perceived flaws and shortcomings. By shifting your focus to your positive attributes and achievements, you can cultivate a more compassionate and nurturing relationship with yourself. This shift in perspective can have a profound impact on your overall well-being and mental health.

By staying true to who you are, you open yourself up to opportunities that align with your genuine interests and passions. This alignment increases the likelihood of finding success and satisfaction in various aspects of life, whether in personal relationships, career pursuits, or creative endeavors. Authentic living encourages you to take risks and explore new possibilities, leading to a richer and more fulfilling life experience.

Incorporating authenticity into daily life requires ongoing reflection and commitment. It is essential to regularly check in with yourself and assess whether your actions align with your true self. This practice can involve journaling, meditation, or simply taking quiet moments to contemplate your intentions and choices. By making authenticity a priority, you reinforce its importance and integrate it more deeply into your everyday existence.

While the journey to living true to oneself may not always be easy, the rewards are worth the effort. Embracing your unique traits and fostering self-acceptance can transform your life in profound ways. It empowers you to live with greater confidence, resilience, and joy. By being true to yourself, you pave the way for a more authentic and fulfilling existence, enriching not only your own life but also the lives of those around you.

Embracing authenticity involves an ongoing journey of personal exploration and development.

Navigating Societal Expectations and Making Decisions Based on Inner Truth

Embodying an authentic self requires a mindful approach to navigating societal pressures and making decisions that resonate with one's inner truths and values. Achieving this alignment involves several strategies that can guide individuals on their journeys toward self-discovery and personal growth.

Setting Personal Boundaries

One fundamental aspect of living authentically is setting personal boundaries. These boundaries act as protective barriers that safeguard our sense of self, ensuring that we do not compromise our values or well-being for the sake of others. Establishing clear limits in our relationships, professional environments, and daily interactions helps maintain our authenticity.

To set effective personal boundaries, begin by identifying what is non-negotiable in your life. This might include respecting your time, preserving your mental health, or upholding core values. Once these areas are defined, communicate them assertively yet kindly to those around you. For instance, if you need alone time to recharge, let friends and family know that you require specific hours of solitude each day.

It is also essential to recognize when boundaries are being overstepped. Pay attention to feelings of discomfort, resentment, or exhaustion—these emotions often signal that your limits are being tested. In such moments, reaffirm your boundaries calmly but firmly. Over time, this practice will cultivate an environment where your true self can thrive without undue pressure or interference.

Cultivating Self-Compassion

Another critical component of authentic living is cultivating self-compassion. This involves treating ourselves with the same kindness and understanding that we would offer a close friend. Embracing mistakes and imperfections as natural facets of the human experience allows us to grow and learn without harsh self-criticism.

Self-compassion can be nurtured through mindfulness practices, such as meditation or journaling. These activities create space for introspection, helping us become more aware of our thoughts and emotions. When faced with setbacks or perceived flaws, resist the urge to judge yourself harshly. Instead, acknowledge your feelings and remind yourself that everyone encounters challenges.

For example, if you make a mistake at work, rather than berating yourself, recognize it as an opportunity to improve. Reflect on what went wrong and how you can address similar situations in the future. By adopting a compassionate mindset, you foster resilience and a deeper connection with your authentic self.

Listening to Intuition

Trusting our intuition is another vital strategy for making decisions aligned with our inner truths. Intuition is that inner voice or gut feeling that guides us toward choices that resonate with who we truly are. Learning to listen to and trust this inner guidance can lead to more fulfilling and authentic decision-making.

To cultivate intuitive awareness, start by paying attention to your body's signals. Physical sensations, such as a tight chest or a relaxed stomach, can provide valuable insights into how you feel about a particular situation. Additionally, consider incorporating regular quiet time into your routine, free from distractions, to tune into your inner voice.

When faced with a decision, take a moment to reflect inwardly. Ask yourself how each option aligns with your values and long-term goals. Often, the choice that feels most authentic will resonate deeply within you, providing a sense of clarity and peace. Trusting this process strengthens your connection to your true self and empowers you to navigate life's complexities with confidence.

Reflecting on Core Values

Finally, reflecting on core values plays a crucial role in living authentically. Our values serve as guiding principles that shape our actions and decisions. By consistently aligning our choices with these values, we ensure that our lives remain true to who we are at our core.

Start by identifying your core values through self-reflection exercises. Consider what matters most to you—be it honesty, compassion, creativity, or any other principle. Write down these values and keep them visible as a constant reminder of what drives you.

Regularly evaluate your decisions and actions against your core values. For example, if you value integrity, assess whether your behavior at work or in personal relationships reflects honesty and transparency. If discrepancies arise, take proactive steps to realign your actions with your values.

Engage in meaningful conversations with trusted friends or mentors to gain different perspectives on your values and how they influence your life. Sharing your reflections can provide valuable insights and reinforce your commitment to living authentically.

Final Insights

Living in alignment with our true selves involves embracing authenticity, setting personal boundaries, cultivating self-compassion, trusting our intuition, and reflecting on our core values. These actions form the foundation for a life that honors who we are at our deepest level. By acknowledging our unique traits and making decisions that resonate with our inner truths, we foster a sense of fulfillment and purpose. This journey requires ongoing reflection and commitment; however, the rewards are profound, leading to a more meaningful connection with ourselves and others.

As you continue on this path, remember to be gentle with yourself. Embrace the process of self-discovery with openness and curiosity, knowing that each step taken toward authenticity brings you closer to genuine happiness and fulfillment. Living authentically invites positive experiences and attracts like-minded individuals who support your growth. By staying true to who you are, you create a life filled with joy, resilience, and deeper connections, enriching your existence and the lives of those around you.

Chapter Nine

Facing and Accepting Change

Embracing change is the first step toward unlocking your true potential and discovering the new opportunities that await you. Human beings often resist change, which can be intimidating and challenging. It shakes the ground beneath us and can create feelings of uncertainty. People tend to cling to their established habits, as these habits create a sense of comfort and familiarity in our lives. When faced with the idea of making changes, even positive ones, individuals may feel a natural pushback.

Throughout the chapter, readers will explore strategies for overcoming the intrinsic fear associated with change. These strategies include shifting perspectives from avoidance to curiosity, which opens up pathways for personal growth and transformation. The chapter also discusses the significance of breaking free from limiting beliefs that hinder progress and how cultivating a growth mindset can turn challenges into opportunities. Practical guidelines such as journaling, positive affirmations, mindfulness techniques, and seeking support from trusted individuals are presented as tools to navigate change more gracefully. Ultimately, this chapter aims to empower readers to view change not as a threat but as a catalyst for ongoing development and self-discovery.

Overcoming resistance to change introduces uncertainty and disrupts familiar patterns. This fear of the unknown can create a sense of discomfort, leading individuals to cling to what is familiar, even if it no longer serves their best interests. For example, someone may stay in an unfulfilling job or relationship simply because they fear the uncertainty of finding something new. By acknowledging this tendency, we can begin to see how our resistance might be holding us back.

Moreover, recognizing that this resistance stems from a place of fear can help us approach it with compassion rather than judgment. Everyone experiences fear when faced with the unknown; it's a natural response. However, understanding that this fear doesn't have to dictate our actions can be empowering. It's about shifting our perspective from one of avoidance to one of curiosity and openness. This shift can pave the way for significant personal transformation as we learn to navigate change with more grace.

Breaking free from limiting beliefs is another crucial step in embracing change. These beliefs often manifest as internal dialogues that tell us we are not capable of more than what we currently have or where we currently are. They can be deeply ingrained, sometimes stemming from childhood experiences or past failures. Challenging these beliefs requires a conscious effort to recognize and reframe them. For instance, if you believe that you are not good enough to pursue a particular career, start by identifying concrete evidence to the contrary—such as past accomplishments or skills you've developed over time.

Guidelines for breaking free from limiting beliefs can include practices such as journaling to identify negative self-talk, engaging in positive affirmations, and seeking feedback from trusted friends or mentors who can offer a more objective view of your capabilities. By actively working to dismantle these limiting beliefs, you open up space for new possibilities and allow yourself to grow beyond previously self-imposed boundaries.

Embracing uncertainty is another vital aspect of navigating change effectively. Change inherently comes with a degree of unpredictability, and trying to control every outcome can lead to anxiety and stress. Developing a mindset of openness and adaptability helps in dealing with this uncertainty. For example, when faced with a sudden job loss, instead of fixating on the perceived negative aspects, look for new opportunities that this change might bring. Perhaps it's a chance to explore a long-forgotten passion or pivot to a different career path that aligns more closely with your values.

To facilitate this mindset shift, consider implementing guidelines such as practicing mindfulness techniques that help anchor you in the present moment. Mindfulness can reduce anxiety about future uncertainties and increase your ability to handle unexpected changes with calm and poise. Another practical guideline is to set flexible goals rather than rigid ones. Flexible goals provide direction but also allow room for adjustments as circumstances evolve, making it easier to navigate the ebbs and flows of change without feeling overwhelmed.

Cultivating a growth mindset is another powerful tool in embracing change as a catalyst for growth. A growth mindset is the belief that abilities and intelligence can be developed through effort, learning, and perseverance. When you view challenges as opportunities for growth, you become more resilient and willing to take risks. Consider the example of learning a new skill. If you approach it with a fixed mindset—believing that you're either naturally good at it or you're not—you may give up quickly if you encounter difficulties. In contrast, a growth mindset encourages you to persist, understanding that effort and practice will lead to improvement over time.

Adopting a growth mindset involves reframing failure as a learning experience rather than a setback. Each obstacle becomes a stepping stone toward greater self-improvement. Celebrating small victories along the way can also reinforce this mindset. For instance, if you're learning to play a musical instrument, acknowledge and celebrate each milestone, whether it's mastering a new chord or playing a simple song. These small successes build confidence and motivate further progress.

Finding inner stability and peace during times of transition and change is crucial for navigating life's inevitable shifts. Cultivating inner grounding practices can provide the foundation needed to stay centered. Techniques such as meditation, breathwork, and mindfulness offer powerful tools for anchoring oneself amid turbulence.

Meditation allows the mind to settle and focus, creating a space where thoughts can be observed without attachment. By dedicating even a few minutes each day to this practice, one can develop a greater sense of calm and clarity. Similarly, breathwork exercises help regulate the nervous system, promoting relaxation and reducing stress. Simple practices such as deep belly breathing or alternate nostril breathing can be incredibly effective in calming the mind and body.

Mindfulness, the practice of being fully present in the moment, encourages a non-judgmental awareness of one's thoughts, feelings, and surroundings. This state of presence can reduce anxiety about the future and regrets about the past, allowing an individual to experience life as it unfolds. Engaging in activities like mindful walking, eating, or even washing dishes can cultivate this practice in everyday life.

Connecting with a sense of purpose is another vital aspect of maintaining stability during times of change. By aligning with core values and passions, individuals can navigate transitions with clarity and direction. Understanding what truly matters can act as a compass, guiding decisions and actions even when external circumstances are uncertain.

To find this sense of purpose, it can be helpful to reflect on what brings joy and fulfillment. Journaling about personal values, interests, and long-term goals can uncover what resonates deeply within. Engaging in activities that align with these discovered purposes, whether it's volunteering for a cause, pursuing a hobby, or fostering relationships, can create a strong internal foundation. When life's changes seem overwhelming, returning to these core values provides a sense of continuity and direction.

Seeking support and guidance is essential during turbulent times. Utilizing available resources, connecting with the community, and prioritizing self-care can fortify one's resilience. Isolation can amplify feelings of instability, so reaching out to friends, family, or support groups can provide comfort and perspective. Sharing experiences and listening to others' stories can normalize feelings of uncertainty and reduce the burden of facing change alone.

Professional guidance from therapists, coaches, or mentors can also offer valuable insights and coping strategies. These professionals can provide tools for managing stress, processing emotions, and developing action plans tailored to individual needs. In addition to seeking external support, creating a self-care routine is fundamental. Regular exercise, adequate sleep, and a balanced diet contribute to overall well-being and enhance one's capacity to handle change.

Embracing the unknown with curiosity is an empowering approach to navigating transitions. Rather than viewing change with fear, approaching it with a mindset of exploration and growth can open new possibilities. Curiosity invites questions such as "What can I learn from this?" or "How might this experience shape my future?" This shift in perspective transforms challenges into opportunities for discovery.

Cultivating curiosity involves practicing openness and flexibility. It means acknowledging fears but choosing to move forward anyway, trusting in one's ability to adapt and grow. Engaging in new experiences, meeting different people, and stepping outside of comfort zones can all foster a sense of curiosity. By welcoming the unknown as a teacher, one can develop resilience and adaptability, essential qualities for thriving in an ever-changing world.

Final Insights

In conclusion, embracing change as a catalyst for growth begins with acknowledging the resistance that often accompanies it. We have explored how the fear of the unknown can keep us stuck in unfulfilling situations and how approaching our fears with compassion can help us overcome this resistance. By shifting our perspective from avoidance to curiosity, we can pave the way for personal transformation. Additionally, challenging limiting beliefs through practices like journaling and positive affirmations opens up new possibilities. Adopting a mindset of openness and adaptability helps manage the unpredictability that change brings, allowing us to navigate life's transitions with greater ease.

Developing a growth mindset is essential for making the most of these changes. When we view challenges as opportunities for learning, we become more resilient and willing to take risks. This mindset shift involves celebrating small victories and seeing failures as learning experiences rather than setbacks. Cultivating inner grounding practices such as meditation, breathwork, and mindfulness can provide the stability needed during times of change. Moreover, aligning with our core values and seeking support can bolster our resilience. By embracing the unknown with curiosity, we can transform challenges into opportunities for discovery and growth, ultimately leading to a more fulfilling and enriched life.

Chapter Ten

The Journey Continues: Living with Purpose

A life infused with purpose sparks a profound and enriching journey of the spirit. In the pages that follow, we will delve into various practices that support the long-term growth of your spiritual journey. These practices include reflection and introspection to filter out distractions and focus on what genuinely matters to you. Setting purposeful goals, fueled by passion, will be discussed as essential steps toward maintaining momentum and motivation. Moreover, sustainable self-care routines and community connections will be explored for their roles in building resilience and fostering a supportive environment. Finally, the importance of generosity and mindfulness will be highlighted, as they enrich your spiritual life, adding layers of joy and compassion to your journey. This chapter aims to provide you with the tools and insights needed to continue your journey with a renewed sense of purpose and fulfillment.

Discovering and Aligning with Your Life Purpose

Embarking on a spiritual journey and aligning with your life purpose can profoundly enhance the experience, providing a sense of direction that is both fulfilling and transformative. Unveiling your deepest desires is an essential first step in this alignment. By understanding what truly moves you at your core, you can begin to see the path forward more clearly. These desires are not just whims or fleeting interests; they are indicators of what will bring you the most satisfaction and fulfillment. When you tap into these deep-seated desires, you unlock a profound sense of purpose, which serves as a beacon guiding you through life's challenges and triumphs.

Reflection plays a critical role in filtering out distractions and focusing on what genuinely resonates with your being. In today's fast-paced world, it's easy to get caught up in the noise of daily life, losing sight of what matters most to you. Taking time for introspection allows you to sift through external influences and internal chatter, helping you identify what holds true meaning. Through reflection, you can hone in on your values, passions, and goals, creating a clearer picture of your life's purpose. This process demands honesty and patience, but the clarity that emerges can make the spiritual journey much more aligned and directed.

Setting goals rooted in your purpose provides the motivation needed for spiritual evolution. Purpose-driven goals differ from ordinary ambitions because they come from a deeper place within you. They are closely tied to your sense of identity and longing, making them incredibly powerful motivators. When you set these kinds of goals, you create a roadmap for your spiritual journey. Each milestone reached not only brings you closer to your ultimate aspiration but also reinforces your sense of purpose and drive. These goals act as stepping stones, helping you navigate your path with intention and conviction. They give structure to your journey, transforming abstract desires into tangible actions.

To effectively set these purposeful goals, consider employing a few guidelines. Start by breaking down your larger vision into smaller, manageable objectives. This makes the journey feel less overwhelming and more achievable. Next, ensure each goal is specific and measurable. Vague aspirations can lead to frustration and confusion, while clear targets help you track progress and stay motivated. Finally, remain flexible and adaptable. The journey toward enlightenment is rarely linear, and being open to adjusting your goals as you grow can prevent stagnation and keep you moving forward.

When your journey is aligned with your passion, your pursuit of enlightenment becomes more meaningful and rewarding. Passion fuels perseverance, providing the energy and enthusiasm needed to overcome obstacles and maintain momentum. When you are passionate about your purpose, the challenges along the way seem less daunting and more like opportunities for growth. Moreover, passion adds a layer of joy and excitement to your spiritual practices, making them something you look forward to rather than a chore. This enthusiasm can be infectious, inspiring those around you and fostering a supportive community of like-minded individuals who share your dedication and drive.

Sustaining Practices for Long-Term Growth

Sustainable practices are essential for continuous growth and evolution on the spiritual path. For many, the journey involves a lifelong commitment to personal development, self-healing, and building meaningful connections with others. Establishing consistent self-care routines forms the foundation of this transformative journey. By nurturing our physical, emotional, and mental well-being, we build resilience and create a stable ground from which we can grow.

Self-care can take many forms, such as regular exercise, mindful meditation, healthy eating, and adequate rest. Simple practices like taking time for a daily walk or engaging in deep-breathing exercises can significantly enhance our sense of well-being. Additionally, journaling thoughts, feelings, and experiences can help process emotions and provide clarity. These small, consistent efforts accumulate over time, fostering a strong and balanced state that supports continued spiritual growth.

An essential aspect of nurturing oneself is learning new things. When we pursue knowledge, whether through reading, attending workshops, or simply exploring new hobbies, we cultivate curiosity and adaptability. This ongoing quest for understanding not only enriches our lives but also helps us stay flexible in the face of change. Being open to new ideas and experiences broadens our perspective and encourages personal development, allowing us to evolve continually.

Moreover, the practice of learning should not be limited to formal education. Embracing new skills, creative pursuits, and hands-on activities can also be incredibly rewarding. Trying out painting, playing a musical instrument, or gardening can stimulate the mind and promote joy. These endeavors serve as reminders that growth can be both enlightening and enjoyable, contributing positively to our spiritual journey.

Community connections play a vital role in supporting sustainable growth on the spiritual path. Building relationships with like-minded individuals provides accountability, inspiration, and shared wisdom. Engaging with a community offers opportunities for mutual support, enabling us to navigate challenges together. Whether through participation in local groups, online forums, or social gatherings, these connections foster a sense of belonging and shared purpose.

Being part of a community also emphasizes the importance of sharing experiences and insights. By openly discussing personal journeys, triumphs, and setbacks, individuals can learn from one another and gain valuable perspectives. This exchange of knowledge helps reinforce our commitments and goals, making the path to spiritual growth less solitary and more collaborative.

Generosity is another powerful sustainer of spiritual evolution. Acts of giving, whether through time, resources, or compassion, create a deep sense of interconnectedness and foster a compassionate outlook toward all beings. Practicing generosity helps us transcend selfish desires and cultivates empathy, thereby enriching our spiritual lives.

When we give without expecting anything in return, we align ourselves with broader universal principles of love and kindness. Volunteering for a cause close to our hearts, offering support to those in need, or simply extending a helping hand to a friend can elevate our spirits and deepen our connection to humanity. These acts of generosity reinforce our sense of purpose and remind us of the greater good we are part of.

To make generosity a sustainable practice, it's helpful to integrate it into our daily routines. Simple actions, such as practicing random acts of kindness, donating to charity, or spending time with someone who needs companionship, can have profound impacts. These gestures, no matter how small, contribute to a ripple effect, spreading positivity and compassion throughout our communities.

Another critical aspect of continuous growth is mindfulness in everyday actions. Mindful self-reflection supports sustainable practices by encouraging awareness and intentional living. Taking time each day to reflect on our thoughts, actions, and intentions fosters a deeper connection with our inner selves. This practice allows us to identify areas for improvement and recognize progress, keeping us aligned with our spiritual goals.

Embracing change is also fundamental to sustained spiritual growth. Evolution on the spiritual path often requires us to let go of old patterns, beliefs, and habits that no longer serve us. Viewing change as an opportunity rather than a threat helps us adapt and thrive. It encourages resilience and flexibility, which are crucial for navigating the challenges and uncertainties life presents.

Seeking feedback from others can further support our evolution. Constructive input from trusted friends, mentors, or community members provides valuable external perspectives. This feedback helps us identify blind spots and areas where we might need to adjust our approach. It also reinforces our commitment to growth and encourages a mindset of continuous improvement.

In conclusion, sustainable practices are the backbone of a fulfilling and evolving spiritual journey. Consistent self-care routines nurture resilience and well-being, creating a stable foundation for growth. Learning new things cultivates curiosity, adaptability, and personal development, enhancing our capacity to thrive. Community connections provide accountability, inspiration, and shared wisdom, fostering a sense of belonging and collective support. Generosity nurtures interconnectedness and compassion, enriching our spiritual lives and reinforcing our sense of purpose.

Final Insights

Continuing the spiritual journey with a sense of purpose involves deeply understanding and aligning with what drives you at your core. By focusing on your deepest desires and reflecting on what truly resonates with you, you can set purposeful goals that guide your path. This alignment requires patience and honesty but provides clarity and direction, making each step on your journey feel intentional and fulfilling. The act of setting purposeful goals transforms abstract desires into tangible actions, helping you navigate your spiritual journey with confidence and conviction.

Sustaining this journey necessitates consistent self-care and a commitment to personal growth. Engaging in regular practices that nurture your physical, emotional, and mental well-being builds resilience and a stable foundation for continued evolution. Connecting with like-minded individuals further enriches this path, offering support and shared wisdom. Acts of generosity also play a crucial role in deepening our connection to humanity, fostering empathy and compassion. Embracing change and seeking feedback help us stay adaptable and committed to our growth. Through these efforts, we create a meaningful and rewarding spiritual journey, grounded in purpose and sustained by continuous reflection and growth.

Conclusion

R eflecting on this journey, it is essential to see how far you have come. From the initial call to embark on your path of spiritual transformation, each chapter has been a step toward embracing your wounds, cultivating self-love, practicing mindfulness, and connecting with your inner wisdom. This book aims to guide you through a comprehensive exploration of self-discovery and healing from within.

In the beginning, you faced the daunting task of understanding your motivations and the core reasons for your pursuit of spiritual growth. Through insightful reflections, you learned to identify emotional pain and uncovered the roots of those feelings. You were encouraged to be gentle with yourself, recognizing that these wounds were part of your human experience. Embracing them was an act of courage and acceptance.

As you progressed, cultivating self-love emerged as a central theme. It wasn't about mere self-esteem or superficial regard; it was about a deep-seated acceptance of who you are at your core. By learning to love and accept yourself unconditionally, you unlocked the potential for profound healing and inner peace. This self-love became the cornerstone upon which all other practices and insights were built.

Practicing mindfulness was another significant part of your journey. Learning to stay present in the moment allowed you to connect deeply with your experiences, fostering a better understanding of yourself. Mindfulness helped you observe your thoughts and emotions without judgment, making it possible to navigate life's complexities with a greater sense of ease and compassion.

Connecting with your inner wisdom was a transformative experience. It guided you toward realizing that every answer you seek lies within you. By quieting external noise and tuning into your intuition, you established a dialogue with your higher self. This connection empowered you to make decisions aligned with your true purpose and values, leading to a more fulfilling life.

The importance of self-love cannot be overstated. It is a recurring message throughout this book because of its transformative power. By loving and accepting yourself, you pave the way for healing and peace. Self-love is not just an abstract concept but a real, practical foundation for personal growth. It influences how you interact with the world, face challenges, and engage in relationships.

Now, as you stand at the threshold of continued growth, it is crucial to incorporate these spiritual practices into your daily routine. Growth is not a one-time event but a continuous process. Integrate what you've learned—whether it's engaging in regular meditation, maintaining a journal, or setting aside time for introspection. These practices will sustain your journey and ensure long-term personal development and fulfillment.

Life is full of challenges, yet each obstacle is an opportunity for growth. By viewing challenges as stepping stones, you foster resilience and wisdom. Embrace change and understand that impermanence is a natural part of life's flow. Adaptability will allow you to navigate transitions gracefully and with purpose. Each challenge you face equips you with new skills and insights, reinforcing your ability to pursue your spiritual journey with strength and determination.

Gratitude plays a pivotal role in this process. By expressing gratitude for the lessons learned and acknowledging your inner strength, you illuminate your path. Gratitude helps you see beauty in both your progress and your trials. Take a moment to reflect on what you are grateful for as you reach the end of this book. Gratitude shifts your perspective, allowing you to recognize the richness of your journey and the growth you have achieved.

Stepping into your authentic self marks the culmination of your journey. It means living a life aligned with who you truly are, beyond societal expectations or superficial identities. Imagine standing in front of a mirror and seeing not just your reflection but your true essence shining through. How will you embrace and embody your authentic self starting today? Empower yourself to live authentically, honoring your true desires and values.

Embarking on a spiritual journey begins with recognizing the internal signals that guide you toward deeper understanding and fulfillment. Acknowledging feelings of inner discontent, discomfort, and emotional emptiness serves as powerful catalysts for personal growth. Embrace these emotions, reflect on their origins, and seek ways to address them constructively. Cultivating curiosity and remaining open to self-discovery can uncover profound insights, leading to meaningful transformations and a more purposeful existence.

Confronting fears and stepping into the unknown is often part of this path. It requires courage and a willingness to be vulnerable. Engaging in practices like mindfulness and introspection helps manage uncertainties, fostering inner peace and resilience. Trust in your journey, even without full certainty. Authentic exploration and growth occur when you step into the unknown with an open heart. Setting clear intentions and aligning actions with core values helps navigate your quest with clarity and determination, ultimately finding greater connection and fulfillment along the way.

As you close this book, remember that your journey doesn't end here. Carry forward the lessons learned, and continue nurturing your spiritual practices. By doing so, you will evolve, adapt, and flourish. Embrace your authenticity, live aligned with your true self, and let your journey of self-discovery unfold with grace and purpose. The path ahead is bright, and the world awaits the unique light you have to offer.

References

- https://www.quora.com/As-spiritual-problem-what-does-emptiness-actually-means-How-does-it-feel

- https://www.quora.com/What-are-the-signs-of-spiritual-emptiness

- https://www.quora.com/What-are-some-signs-of-spiritual-awakening-I-have-been-feeling-disconnected-from-my-physical-body-and-I-feel-no-desire-to-participate-in-the-physical-world-it-feels-weird-and-someone-said-that-it-is-me-being

- https://mariaerving.com/aloneness-on-spiritual-path/

- https://www.quora.com/How-can-one-overcome-the-constant-feeling-of-spiritual-emptiness

- https://www.verywellmind.com/how-to-find-emotional-healing-5214462

- https://www.forbes.com/sites/margiewarrell/2018/09/15/still-not-happy-why-embracing-your-painful-emotions-makes-people-happier/

- https://psychcentral.com/blog/how-to-deal-with-emotional-pain

- https://greatergood.berkeley.edu/article/item/four_ways_we_avoid_our_feelings_and_what_to_do_instead

- https://www.mayoclinic.org/healthy-lifestyle/adult-health/in-depth/forgiveness/art-20047692

- https://livethepain.org/radical-acceptance-why-should-i-embrace-my-pain/https://www.quora.com/What-is-the-void-stage-in-spiritual-awakening

- https://self-compassion.org/blogs-category-fierce-self-compassion/

- https://self-compassion.org/the-program/

- https://changesbigandsmall.com/how-to-embrace-self-acceptance-and-cultivate-self-compassion/

- https://self-compassion.org/exercises/exercise-2-self-compassion-break/

- https://self-compassion.org/self-compassion-test/

- https://self-compassion.org/

- https://positivepsychology.com/mindfulness-exercises-techniques-activities/

- https://www.mayoclinic.org/healthy-lifestyle/consumer-health/in-depth/mindfulness-exercises/art-20046356

- https://newsinhealth.nih.gov/2021/06/mindfulness-your-health

- https://www.mindful.org/how-to-manage-stress-with-mindfulness-and-meditation/

- https://www.hawaiipacifichealth.org/healthier-hawaii/live-healthy/8-mindfulness-exercises-that-also-reduce-stress/

- https://psychcentral.com/lib/change-how-you-feel-change-how-you-breathe

- https://peelyork.bigbrothersbigsisters.ca/wp-content/uploads/sites/160/2018/04/Exercises-for-Emotion-Regulation-1.pdf

- https://manahealthclinic.com.au/the-benefits-of-breathwork-for-emotional-regulation/

- https://www.webmd.com/balance/stress-management/stress-relief-breathing-techniques

- https://www.healthline.com/health/breathing-exercise

- https://www.nhs.uk/mental-health/self-help/guides-tools-and-activities/breathing-exercises-for-stress/

- https://peermag.org/articles/embracing-your-worth/

- https://www.on-curating.org/issue-44-reader/affirmative-critique.html

- https://skylight.org/blog/posts/affirmations-for-self-esteem-and-why-they-work

- https://acendahealth.org/the-power-of-positive-affirmations/

- https://ed.stanford.edu/sites/default/files/annurev-psych-psychology_of_change_final_e2.pdf

- https://booksbywomen.org/jane-enbright-on-positive-thinking-and-affirmations/

- https://www.proctorgallagherinstitute.com/24913/difference-between-intuition-and-ego

- https://www.quora.com/How-can-someone-differentiate-between-their-higher-self-and-ego-when-making-intuitive-decisions

- https://www.quora.com/Why-cant-I-tell-the-difference-between-my-intuition-ego-and-desire-What-am-I-doing-wrong

- https://www.quora.com/How-can-we-differentiate-between-the-voice-of-ego-and-intuition-on-our-spiritual-path

- https://www.quora.com/How-do-you-distinguish-ego-voice-and-intuition
- https://www.quora.com/How-can-you-differentiate-between-intuition-and-imagination-ego-How-can-you-determine-which-one-to-act-on
- https://executive.berkeley.edu/thought-leadership/blog/importance-authenticity
- https://trustmentalhealth.com/blog/the-power-of-authenticity-embracing-your-true-self
- https://www.resiliencetraining.co.uk/understanding-and-embracing-your-authentic-self/
- https://www.linkedin.com/pulse/embracing-authenticity-power-being-yourself-thomas-abraham-p-rkwic
- https://www.linkedin.com/pulse/embracing-authenticity-key-living-fulfilling-life-ashish-joshi-i9o6f
- https://www.channelkindness.org/embracing-authenticity/
- https://www.linkedin.com/pulse/embracing-change-your-path-personal-growth-sharad-koche-fbjcf
- https://thetherapycentre.ca/embracing-change-guide-growth-resilience/
- https://medium.com/@mazior_nyanyo/embracing-change-a-journey-towards-personal-growth-and-success-32a5efdo69d
- https://wellbeingstrategist.com/create-wellbeing-change-in-order-to-grow/
- https://www.reached.co.nz/change-and-growth-a-river-runs-through-it/
- https://sotxcounseling.com/embracing-change-strategies-for-personal-growth-and-transformation/

- https://cac.org/daily-meditations/life-as-a-spiritual-journey-weekly-summary/

- https://www.linkedin.com/pulse/cultivating-spiritual-growth-through-daily-habits-rev-michael-pdgsc

- https://jonathanmpham.com/en/spirituality/practices/spiritual-activities/

- https://www.bookbaker.com/fr/v/Elevate-A-Guide-to-Personal-Growth-and-Stress-Management-Spiritual-Growth-and-Connection-with-God/8a323d33-d326-4ace-ad22-ac3b95c43ce5/7

- https://www.sanctuaryonchurch.org/daily-life-a-spiritual-journey

- https://www.linkedin.com/pulse/dont-miss-out-living-your-best-life-discover-purpose-now-k-c-barr-ctl8e

Biography

About the Author

Misty Summers — a cosmic wanderer with a stethoscope and a penchant for moonlit meditations — was born in Vietnam, where the ancient temples, resilient spirits, and lush rice fields whispered secrets about the universe. In 1981, she folded her dreams into a paper crane and flew across oceans to the land of skyscrapers and pumpkin spice lattes. Southern California became her enchanted realm, where she navigated complexities, learned resilience, and found glimpses of the sacred in everyday life. How often have you sought refuge from external disturbances, only to discover that they echo your inner landscape? In Misty's world, every challenge is a spell to be broken, and every moment is a chance to find magic in the mundane.

Offshore medical school beckoned, promising scalpel-wielding adventures. But fate, that mischievous trickster, had other plans. A chronic condition sidestepped her career like a cat avoiding a puddle. The white coat she had longed to wear now hung forgotten, replaced by resilience and an unwavering spirit.

Undeterred, *Misty* pirouetted into the corporate tango. Health information technology became her jam—the binary waltz of ones and zeros, the PowerPoint slides that muttered, "You're not a doctor, but you can still cure Excel errors." She mastered spreadsheets like a wizard, casting spells to summon quarterly reports.

Yet, beneath fluorescent lights, she felt the cosmic itch. The mundane morphed into the mystical. She traded her ergonomic chair for a meditation cushion, her inbox for divine synchronicities. The ego, that clingy roommate, packed its bags and moved out. Her soul threw a housewarming party, and the universe RSVP'd with stardust confetti.

Today, *Misty* weaves her experiences into prose, inviting readers to explore the sacred terrain of the human heart. Her words ripple across time and space like laughter in a mystic river. "Death of the ego?" she chuckles. "More like 'Ego, take a nap and stop hogging the Wi-Fi.'" "Enlightenment for Dummies: A User-Friendly Guide," sits on cosmic bookshelves, right next to "Quantum Physics for Cats."

So, dear readers, join Misty on her mystical journey. Enlightenment awaits, wrapped in a punchline and sprinkled with moonbeams. And remember, the universe has a sense of humor— it's just waiting for you to get the punchline.